Joseph H. Dampier's

Workbook on
Christian
Doctrine

New International Edition

for Teens and Adults

edited by
Charles W. Craig, Jr.

STANDARD
PUBLISHING
Cincinnati, Ohio

ISBN 0-87403-178-8

Contents

HOW TO USE THIS BOOK

WORKBOOK: A student's individual exercise book of problems to be solved directly on the pages.

—Webster's New Collegiate Dictionary

This is a "help yourself" book. The purpose of this book is to provide the guidance necessary for you to "help yourself" discover spiritual truth. The premise of this book is "don't tell a student something he can learn for himself." We learn best and remember the longest what we learn for ourselves.

The only resources you will need to take along on this journey to first-hand Biblical knowledge is a Bible and a dictionary. With just these two resources (along with a pencil and some time) you will be able to answer most of the questions in this book. A few questions pertaining to your local church may require some help from your minister or teacher.

At the end of each lesson is a list of words to be looked up in the dictionary. These are words that are used in the Bible and also in sermons and conversations about spiritual things. They are words with which you ought to be familiar. One way to be sure that you will remember the definitions of these words is to begin using them as soon as possible in answering questions in a later lesson.

Note: The vocabulary and spelling in this workbook follow the *New International Version* of the Bible.

SUGGESTIONS FOR TEACHERS

While this workbook is intended primarily for individual use, it can also be used in a large group setting. It may be used with profit either for an inquirers class or a new members class that focuses on the basic teachings of Scripture.

With some creative planning by the teacher, this book can provide a basic course in Christian doctrine for either youth or adults in a variety of settings. It could be used as an elective Sunday school class; as a part of basic teacher training; as a youth Bible study guide; or even in a summer camp or retreat setting.

The purpose of the book is to encourage those who use it to read their Bibles and work out solutions to the problems for themselves. After having done this (perhaps before the class session) students could be led in a discussion focusing on application of the Biblical truth to life.

Supplementary material for teachers who desire to use this book in a class setting may be found in *The Family of God*, and *The New Testament Church: Then and Now*, by LeRoy Lawson.

Teachers would do well to work through the entire book on their own as well as consult the supplementary materials before attempting to structure class sessions around this material.

1
Sin

1. What is sin? (1 John 3:4; 1 John 5:17)

_____

_____

2. How many have sinned? (1 John 1:8-10; Romans 3:23)

_____

_____

3. When and where was sin introduced into the human family? (Genesis 3:1-19)

_____

_____

4. Who introduced it? (Genesis 3:1-6)

(1) _____

(2) _____

(3) _____

5. How does Genesis 3:1-6 relate to 1 John 3:4?

_____

_____

_____

6. What are some of the consequences of sin? (Romans 6:23; Genesis 3:14-19)

(1) _____

(2) _____

(3) _____

(4) _____

(5) _____

7. Who did Jesus say was the master and father of those who live in sin? (John 8:34, 44)

_____

_____

8. What is the fruit of sin? (Romans 7:5; Galatians 6:7, 8)

_____

_____

9. Is the Christian always at war with sin? (Romans 7:15-24; Galatians 5:17)

_____

_____

10. Does God know all about sin? (Luke 16:15)

_____

_____

11. What is the final punishment for unforgiven sin? (Luke 13:27, 28; Matthew 7:23; Revelation 20:14, 15)

_____

_____

12. What causes a person to sin? (Matthew 13:24, 25 and 38, 39; James 1:14; 4:1, 2)

_____

_____

_____

13. How can one sin by doing nothing at all? (James 4:17)

_____

_____

_____

14. How are we to overcome sin? (James 4:7; Hebrews 2:18; 4:15; 12:3, 4; Ephesians 6:11-17; Romans 12:21)

_____

_____

_____

15. What does resisting temptation do for us? (James 1:2-4; 1 Peter 1:6, 7)

_____

_____

16. Can Christians successfully resist temptation? (1 Corinthians 10:13)

_____

_____

17. Are they always successful in resisting temptations? (Acts 8:18-24; Matthew 26:69-75)

_____

_____

_____

18. What must the Christian do when he sins? (Matthew 26:75; Acts 8:22)

_____

_____

_____

19. What is the hope of forgiveness of sins? (Matthew 1:21)

_____

_____

_____

Key Words

Use a dictionary and find meaning for the following words:

Iniquity _____

_____

Trespass _____

_____

Transgression _____

_____

2
Forgiveness of Sin

1. Define the word "forgiveness."

_____

_____

_____

2. In the Old Testament, what was the basis of forgiveness of sin? (Leviticus 4:6-10, 20)

_____

_____

_____

3. What is the basis of forgiveness in the New Testament? (Matthew 26:28; 1 John 1:7)

_____

_____

_____

_____

_____

4. Who has been given the power to forgive sin? (Mark 2:3-12)

(1) _____

_____

(2) _____

_____

5. Why did God plan for the forgiveness of sins? (John 3:16; 1 John 4:10)

_____

_____

_____

6. Are we ever good enough to deserve the forgiveness of sins? (Romans 5:6-8; Ephesians 2:8-10)

_____

_____

7. Is there any salvation promised except through Christ? (Acts 4:12)

_____

_____

8. Does God offer salvation on some particular terms? (Hebrews 7:25)

_____

_____

9. What are some of the terms?

(1) Romans 5:1; Acts 16:31. _____

_____

_____

_____

(2) Acts 2:38. _____

_____

_____

_____

(3) Matthew 10:32. _____

_____

_____

_____

(4) Mark 16:16. _____

_____

_____

_____

Add any other conditions. _____

_____

_____

10. Will forgiven sins be remembered in judgment? (Acts 3:19; Hebrews 8:12)

_____

_____

_____

11. Can sins that are committed after accepting Christ be forgiven? (1 John 1:9; Hebrews 10:17, 18; 1 Peter 5:7, 8)

_____

_____

_____

_____

Key Words

Use a dictionary and find meaning for the following words:

Messiah _____

_____

_____

Christian _____

_____

_____

Antichrist _____

_____

_____

Blasphemy _____

_____

_____

3
The Gospel

1. What is the gospel? (Romans 1:16)

_____

_____

2. What are the chief elements of the gospel?

Facts
- (1) _____
- (2) _____
- (3) _____

To be believed.

Commands
- (1) _____
- (2) _____
- (3) _____

To be obeyed.

Promises
- (1) _____
- (2) _____
- (3) _____

To be enjoyed.

(If you have any trouble filling in the spaces above, read 1 Corinthians 15:1-5; Acts 2:38 and John 3:16.)

3. How did men and women become Christians in the first churches?

	Facts Believed	Commands Obeyed	Promises Enjoyed
Acts 2:37-41			
Acts 3:19			
Acts 8:5-12			
Acts 8:26-38			
Acts 16:28-34			
Acts 18:6-8			

(Note: Not every one of the above cases mentions "facts," "commands," or "promises.")

4. If the apostles of Jesus were content to make Christians in this way, have we any right to ask more (or less)?

_____

_____

_____

5. If obedient believers received the Holy Spirit in New Testament times, is it not true that they receive the Spirit today?

_____

_____

Key Words
Use your dictionary and find the meaning of the following words:

Justification _____

_____

Fellowship _____

_____

Righteousness _____

_____

Hypocrite _____

_____

4
Faith

1. What is the dictionary definition of faith?

_____

_____

2. Define faith according to Hebrews 11:1.

_____

_____

3. How do we obtain faith? (Romans 10:13, 14, 17)

_____

_____

4. Did Christ seek faith in His followers when here on earth? Give some instances. (Matthew 9:22; John 11:25; Matthew 8:10; John 12:36)

(1) _____

(2) _____

(3) _____

(4) _____

5. What did Jesus ask us to believe? (John 14:1; John 7:38; John 5:24; John 3:14-18)

_____

_____

6. How did His followers state this faith? (Matthew 16:16; John 11:27)

_____

_____

7. What were some of the things that Jesus promised to those who believe?

(1) In Mark 9:23 _____

_____

(2) In Mark 16:16 _____

_____

(3) In John 1:12 _____

_____

11

(4) In John 3:16 _____

_____

(5) In John 3:18 _____

_____

(6) In John 3:36 and 5:24 _____

_____

(7) In John 12:36 and 46 _____

_____

(8) In John 20:31 _____

_____

8. What did the apostles teach should be the object of our faith?

(1) In Acts 16:34 _____

_____

(2) In 1 John 4:16 _____

_____

(3) In Acts 16:31 _____

_____

(4) In Romans 10:9 _____

_____

(5) In Galatians 2:16 _____

_____

(6) In Romans 3:22 _____

_____

9. What did the apostles of Jesus promise to the believers?

(1) In 1 Timothy 4:10 _____

_____

(2) In 2 Timothy 1:12 _____

_____

(3) In Acts 10:43 _____

_____

(4) In Romans 3:26 _____

_____

(5) In Romans 10:9 _____

_____

(6) In 1 Peter 1:18 _____

_____

(7) In Romans 15:13 _____

_____

(8) In Ephesians 2:8 _____

_____

(9) In Romans 5:1 _____

_____

10. Can one have a living faith without showing it by his life? (Titus 2:14; Matthew 25:34-46; James 2:14-24)

_____

Key Words

Use your dictionary to find the meaning of the following words:

Grace _____

_____

Gospel _____

_____

Sin _____

_____

12

5
Repentance

1. What is the dictionary definition of repentance?

   _____

   _____

   _____

   _____

   _____

2. Is repentance necessary to becoming a Christian? (Luke 13:3; Acts 3:19 and 2 Corinthians 7:10)

   _____

   _____

   _____

3. What should lead us to repent? (Acts 17:30, 31; Luke 10:13, 14; 5:32; Romans 2:4; 2 Corinthians 7:8-11)

   (1) _____

   _____

   (2) _____

   _____

4. What order does Peter give for remission of sins, baptism and repentance? (Acts 2:38)

   (1) _____

   (2) _____

   (3) _____

5. What do we turn from when we repent? (Hebrews 6:1)

_____

_____

6. To whom do we turn when we repent? (Acts 20:21; 1 Peter 2:25)

_____

_____

7. What two things are to be forsaken, according to Isaiah 55:7?

(1) _____

_____

(2) _____

_____

8. What does John the Baptist mean by "fruit worthy of repentance"? (Luke 3:8-14)

_____

_____

_____

_____

9. In the story of the prodigal son (Luke 15:11-32), did he show repentance? When did he repent? How did repentance affect his actions? Did the elder brother repent? Did the latter have anything to repent of?

_____

_____

_____

_____

_____

_____

10. What happens when we repent?

(1) Acts 26:20 _____

_____

(2) Acts 2:38 _____

_____

(3) Acts 3:19 _____

_____

(4) Luke 15:17 _____

_____

11. What happens if we do not repent?

(1) Revelation 2:5 _____

_____

(2) Luke 13:5 _____

_____

12. Is repentance a thing that we do once and for all, or is it a continuing thing to be repeated as often as necessary? (Acts 8:22; Revelation 2:5.)

_____

_____

Key Words

Use your dictionary to find the meaning of the following words:

Epistle _____

_____

Doctrine _____

_____

Law _____

_____

6

Confession

1. Is it necessary for us to make a public confession of our faith when we become believers? (Matthew 10:32)

_____

_____

_____

2. Is this confession of faith a condition of salvation? (Romans 10:9)

_____

_____

_____

3. How did Peter state this faith? (Matthew 16:16)

_____

_____

_____

4. What did Jesus say was the origin of this confession? (Matthew 16:17)

_____

_____

_____

5. What did Jesus promise would be built on this faith? (Matthew 16:18)

_____

_____

_____

6. What did Jesus promise to those who would confess Him? (Matthew 10:32)

_____

_____

_____

7. What did Jesus say of those who disowned Him? (Matthew 10:33)

_____

_____

_____

8. Is every person either confessing or denying Christ? (John 3:18; Matthew 12:30)

_____

_____

_____

9. What reason, other than unbelief, has prevented men from publicly confessing their faith in Christ? (John 12:42, 43)

_____

_____

_____

10. How can our lives be a testimony to our faith in Christ? (Luke 8:39; 1 Peter 3:15; Acts 4:13; Matthew 5:14-16)

_____

_____

_____

_____

11. If our life is not in keeping with our confession, will the confession be acceptable? (Matthew 7:21)

_____

_____

_____

_____

12. What is our confession if we do not seek to do the will of God? (1 John 1:6 and 2:4)

_____

_____

_____

13. What is the result of confessing Christ? (1 John 4:15)

_____

_____

_____

Key Words

Use your dictionary and find the meaning for the following words:

Forgiveness _____

_____

_____

Reconciliation _____

_____

_____

Mediator _____

7
How Baptism Is Performed

1. In a good unabridged dictionary find the meaning of the Greek root of the word "baptism."

_____

_____

_____

2. What language did Jesus and His apostles commonly use?

_____

_____

_____

3. Look up the following references. Find the clues to what form of baptism was used and check in the column the clue that fits the form. Two references are worked out for you, showing how this is done.

Reference	Clues	Pouring	Sprinkling	Immersion
Matthew 3:5, 6	with water	X	X	X
Matthew 3:11				
Matthew 3:16				
Mark 1:5				
John 1:26				
John 1:31-33				
John 3:23				

Reference	Clues	Pouring	Sprinkling	Immersion
Acts 1:5				
Acts 11:16				
Acts 8:36-39				
Acts 10:47				
Acts 22:16	a washing			X
Romans 6:1-6				
1 Corinthians 10:1, 2				
Ephesians 5:26				
Colossians 2:12				
1 Peter 3:21				
Titus 3:5				
Mark 1:8-10				

4. Which form fulfills all the requirements?

_____

_____

5. How many baptisms are there? (Ephesians 4:5)

_____

_____

6. Do you believe that men have a right to change the form of an ordinance when the ordinance is a command of Christ? (Matthew 28:19)

_____

_____

7. Which comes first, belief or baptism? (Acts 2:41; 8:12; 16:31-33; 18:8)

_____

_____

8. Is there any Scripture which teaches that any one who had not yet become a believer (an infant) was baptized?

_____

_____

9. Does Matthew 19:14 or Hebrews 10:22 have any reference to baptism?

_____

_____

10. What is the baptismal formula? (Matthew 28:19)

_____

_____

_____

Key Words

In your dictionary find the meaning of the following words:

Condemnation _____

_____

Sacrifice _____

_____

Pentecost _____

_____

Inspiration _____

8
The Meaning of Baptism

1. With what three divine personalities are we brought in contact by baptism? (Matthew 28:19)

   (1) _____

   _____

   (2) _____

   _____

   (3) _____

   _____

2. What three great facts of Christ's life and work do we show forth in baptism? (Romans 6:4; Colossians 2:12)

   (1) _____

   _____

   (2) _____

   _____

   (3) _____

   _____

3. What three things precede baptism? (Mark 16:16; Acts 2:38; Romans 10:9, 10)

   (1) _____

   _____

   (2) _____

   _____

   (3) _____

   _____

4. What three things are promised after baptism? (Acts 2:38; 22:16; Mark 16:16)

(1) _____

_____

(2) _____

_____

(3) _____

_____

5. Can a man be born again, without baptism? (John 3:5)

_____

_____

6. What things are done away with in baptism? (Romans 6:1-11; Colossians 2:12; 2:13-15)

_____

_____

7. According to the same Scriptures, what are the new things we take on?

_____

_____

8. In what way do you think the act of baptism should change your attitude toward life? In what way should it make your attitude different in the future?

_____

_____

_____

_____

9. Would the neglect of baptism be according to the will of God? (Matthew 3:15)

_____

_____

10. Do the Scriptures make a connection between baptism and forgiveness of sin? (Acts 2:38; 22:16; 1 Peter 3:21)

_____

_____

11. From your study of faith, repentance, confession, etc., do you believe that baptism, without any of these other qualifications, will save one from sin and its consequences?

_____

_____

12. What bearing does your answer to the preceding question have on the baptism of infants?

_____

_____

13. Is baptism a proper qualification for church membership? (Acts 2:41)

_____

14. What bearing does John 15:14 have on baptism?

_____

_____

_____

Key Words

In your dictionary find the meaning of the following words:

Redemption _____

_____

Renewal _____

_____

Salvation _____

_____

9

The
New Testament
Church

1. What names were used for the church in the New Testament? (Acts 20:28; 1 Timothy 3:15; Romans 16:16; 1 Corinthians 14:33; Hebrews 12:23)

   (1) _____

   (2) _____

   (3) _____

   (4) _____

   (5) _____

2. By what names were the members of the churches known as recorded in the New Testament? (Acts 11:26; Colossians 1:2; Philippians 1:1)

   (1) _____

   (2) _____

   (3) _____

   (4) _____

3. How is the relationship of Christ to the church described in the New Testament?

   (1) Ephesians 5:23 _____

   _____

(2) Colossians 1:13 _____

_____

(3) John 13:13 _____

_____

(4) John 15:1-8 _____

_____

(5) 1 Corinthians 3:11, 12 _____

_____

(6) Ephesians 2:20 _____

_____

(7) Matthew 16:18 _____

_____

(8) Revelation 19:7-9; Ephesians 5:22-32 _____

_____

4. Did Christ desire a united church? (John 17:20, 21)

_____

_____

5. Is it a sin to have division in the church? (1 Corinthians 1:10, 11)

_____

_____

6. Is the church a divine or a human institution in its origin? (Matthew 16:15-18; Ephesians 2:20, 22)

_____

7. What are the qualifications of an elder (or bishop) of the church? (1 Timothy 3:1-7)

_____

_____

_____

8. What are some of the duties of an elder? (1 Peter 5:1-3; Acts 20:17, 28, 35)

_____

_____

_____

9. What are some of the obligations of the congregation to an elder? (1 Timothy 5:1, 17, 19; Hebrews 13:7 and 17)

_____

_____

_____

10. What are the qualifications of a deacon? (1 Timothy 3:8-13)

_____

_____

11. What is the work of a deacon? (Acts 6:1-3)

_____

_____

Key Words

Use your dictionary and find the meaning for the following:

Evangel _____

_____

Evangelist _____

_____

Passover _____

_____

Evil _____

_____

10
The Bible

1. How many books are there in the Bible?

_____

2. How many are there in the Old Testament?

_____

3. How many are there in the New Testament?

_____

4. Name two books that received their titles from the names of their authors.

_____

_____

5. Name some books that received their titles from the names of the people to whom they were written.

_____

_____

_____

6. Name some books that received their titles from the nature of their contents.

_____

_____

7. Into what parts is the Bible "rightly divided"?

A _____

Genesis | Exodus | Leviticus | Numbers | Deuteronomy | Joshua | Judges | Ruth | 1 Samuel | 2 Samuel | 1 Kings | 2 Kings | 1 Chronicles | 2 Chronicles | Ezra | Nehemiah | Esther | Job | Psalms | Proverbs | Ecclesiastes | Song of Solomon | Isaiah | Jeremiah | Lamentations | Ezekiel | Daniel | Hosea | Joel | Amos | Obadiah | Jonah | Micah

B _____

First: Take your pencil and draw a line from line A to line B at the place that will divide the books of the Old Testament from the books of the New Testament.

Second: From the top of the books draw a line to line A in such a way as to divide the books into the following groups: Historical Beginnings, Law, Jewish History, Poetry, Jewish Prophecy, Life of Christ, Church History, Epistles, New Testament Prophecy. Write the names of the group in the space above the books.

Third: Extend the lines that divide the books to line B in such a way as to divide the books into three dispensations: The Patriarchal, the Jewish and the Christian. Write the names of the dispensation in the space below the books.

Nahum | Habakkuk | Zephaniah | Haggai | Zechariah | Malachi | Matthew | Mark | Luke | John | Acts | Romans | 1 Corinthians | 2 Corinthians | Galatians | Ephesians | Philippians | Colossians | 1 Thessalonians | 2 Thessalonians | 1 Timothy | 2 Timothy | Titus | Philemon | Hebrews | James | 1 Peter | 2 Peter | 1 John | 2 John | 3 John | Jude | Revelation

8. What does the Bible claim as its original source? (Hebrews 1:1-4)

_____

_____

9. Did the writers of the Bible show their own style of writing in the books that they wrote?

_____

_____

10. Is their message the inspired Word of God? Can it be to us a safe guide by which we can know the will of God? (2 Timothy 3:16; 1 Thessalonians 2:13)

_____

_____

11. Is the revelation of God's will as it is found in the Bible to be changed by men? (Galatians 1:8, 11, 12)

_____

_____

12. Write down some of the things which you must depend upon the Bible to teach you.

_____

_____

_____

_____

Key Words

Use your dictionary to find the meaning of these words:

Pharisee _____   Scribe _____

_____   _____

_____   _____

Sadducee _____   Herodian _____

_____   _____

_____   _____

11

The Covenants
and the Priesthood

[Before attempting to answer these questions you should work the diagram dealing with the covenants on pages 28 and 29.]

1. Did Christ fulfill the law of Moses? (Hebrews 4:15; 1 Peter 2:22)

_____

_____

_____

2. When He fulfilled the law what did He do with it? (Matthew 5:17; Colossians 2:14)

_____

_____

_____

3. What is a mediator? _____

_____

_____

_____

_____

4. Why is Christ spoken of as a mediator? (Hebrews 8:6; 12:24; 1 Timothy 2:5)

_____

_____

_____

5. Distinguish between the old and new covenants.

Scripture References	Who were the parties to this covenant?	What is man's part in order to enjoy the promises?
Exodus 19:1-8 Exodus 24:4-8 Exodus 34:27, 28 Hebrews 8:4-13		
Galatians 3:13-29 Hebrews 8:6; 9:28 Matthew 26:28		

The Bible speaks of many covenants made between individuals and God. The important thing is to distinguish between the two above covenants. If you can do this, you will have properly divided the Old Testament and the New Testament, the Old Covenant and the New

What are God's promises under this covenant?	How was this covenant sealed?	Is this covenant binding on you?

Covenant, and the Law and the Gospel. Notice that the word "Testament" and the word "Covenant" are interchangeable. The term "Law" is usually interchangeable with the "Old" Covenant.

6. With the change of the covenants is there also a change of the priesthood? (Hebrews 7:12)

_____

_____

7. Who is the High Priest of Christians? (Hebrews 9:11; 8:1-3)

_____

_____

8. What sacrifice does He offer for sin? (Hebrews 9:11-14)

_____

_____

9. Who are the priests under this High Priest? (1 Peter 2:9; Revelation 1:6)

_____

_____

10. Can any one now stand between you and God except your High Priest?

_____

11. If you as a believer are now a priest before God, what is your responsibility and what difference does it make in your conduct?

_____

_____

_____

Key Words

Using your dictionary, give the meaning for the following words:

Glory _____

_____

Sanctified _____

_____

Covenant _____

_____

Testament _____

_____

12
The Lord's Supper

1. Who gave us the Lord's Supper? (Matthew 26:17-30; Mark 14:12, 22-24; Luke 22:19, 20; John 13:4; 1 Corinthians 11:23-26)

   _____

   _____

   _____

2. When was it instituted? (See Scriptures in previous question.)

   _____

   _____

   _____

3. What two elements are necessary in the Lord's Supper? (Matthew 26:26-29)

   (1) _____

   (2) _____

4. What do the bread and the fruit of the vine represent?

   _____

   _____

   _____

5. Did the early Christians do as Jesus commanded? (Acts 2:42; 20:7)

   _____

   _____

   _____

6. When did the early Christians observe the Lord's Supper? (Acts 20:7)

   _____

   _____

   _____

7. How often do you think we should partake of the Lord's Supper? (Acts 20:7)

_____

_____

_____

8. Why should we continue to observe this Supper? (1 Corinthians 11:24-30)

_____

_____

_____

9. What names are used in the New Testament for this Supper? (Acts 2:42; 1 Corinthians 10:16; 11:20; 10:21)

    (1) _____

    (2) _____

    (3) _____

    (4) _____

10. Do you know of any place in the Bible that forbids any Christian from serving at the Lord's Table?

_____

_____

_____

11. Who usually serves at the communion table in your church?

_____

_____

_____

12. List some things you should think about when you partake of the emblems. (Matthew 26:28; 1 Corinthians 11:24)

_____

_____

_____

13. Do you think you should silently pray after receiving the emblems?

_____

_____

_____

14. List some suitable parts for such a prayer.

_____

_____

_____

15. What is the result of partaking in an unworthy manner (that is, partaking without discerning the Lord's body)? (1 Corinthians 11:29, 30)

_____

_____

_____

Key Words

Use your dictionary to find the meaning of these words:

Intercession _____

_____

Priest _____

_____

Miracle _____

_____

Prophet _____

_____

13

The Work of
the Holy Spirit

PART I

The Work of the Holy Spirit Through the Apostles of Jesus.

1. What did Jesus promise His apostles as regards the Spirit? (Acts 1:5-8)

_____

_____

_____

2. What were the signs that accompanied the fulfillment of this promise?

_____

_____

_____

3. What was the purpose for these signs? (Hebrews 2:1-4; 1 Corinthians 14:22)

_____

_____

_____

4. What are the qualifications of an apostle? (Acts 1:21, 22)

_____

_____

_____

33

5. Did Paul fulfill the qualifications of being a witness to the resurrection of Jesus? How? (Acts 26:14-16)

_____

_____

6. Did the apostles lay hands on men to give them the power to work miracles? (Acts 8:17)

_____

_____

7. Did any one who was not an apostle ever have this power to lay on hands and give the power to confer miracles? (Acts 6:5; 8:5-8, 14-17)

_____

8. Does the New Testament teach that the power to work miracles is a temporary one in the church? (1 Corinthians 13:8)

_____

_____

PART II

The Holy Spirit Dwells in the Believer.

1. What is better than working miracles? (1 Corinthians 12:31; 13:13)

_____

_____

2. Is the Spirit promised as an indwelling presence to believers? (1 John 3:24; 1 Corinthians 6:19; 1 Thessalonians 4:8; Acts 5:32)

_____

_____

_____

3. What is the fruit of the Spirit in our lives? (Galatians 5:22, 23; 2 Timothy 1:7)

_____

_____

_____

4. Is the fruit of the Spirit the evidence that the Spirit dwells in us, or should we expect some peculiar feeling?

_____

_____

_____

5. What is the means used by the Spirit to do much of His work? (Ephesians 6:17; 1 Peter 1:22, 23)

_____

_____

Key Words

Use your dictionary to find the meaning of these words:

Reveal _____

_____

Inspire _____

_____

Dedicate _____

_____

Consecrate _____

_____

14 Prayer

1. What is the first great truth about God upon which Jesus based His teaching about prayer? (Matthew 5:45; 6:9; 7:11)

_____

_____

_____

2. Is the need of prayer based on the fact that God does not know our needs? (Matthew 6:8)

_____

_____

_____

3. Arrange the following reasons for praying in their order of importance:

Praying to get something we do not have.

Praying that we may keep something we already have.

Praying to give thanks for something we have received.

Praying in order to be more Christlike.

Praying not for our own needs, but the needs of others.

Praying in order that we may have fellowship with God as our Father.

4. Are we promised that our prayers will be answered? (Matthew 7:7-11; Matthew 21:22; Mark 11:24; John 16:23)

_____

_____

_____

5. On what conditions does God fulfill the above promises?

John 14:13_____

_____

Matthew 18:19 _____

_____

John 15:7 _____

_____

James 4:3 _____

_____

1 John 5:14 _____

_____

6. In the prayer life of Jesus, what is the difference in the length of (1) His private prayers (Luke 6:12; Matthew 26:36-44; John 17:1-26) and (2) His public prayers? (Matthew 11:25-27; John 11:41, 42; Luke 23:34)

_____

_____

_____

_____

7. What are some of the things Jesus taught His followers about prayer? (Matthew 6:5-8)

_____

_____

_____

_____

8. In the model prayer that Jesus taught His disciples to pray (Matthew 6:9-13),

How is God addressed?_____

_____

How is God honored?_____

_____

What things do we ask for?_____

_____

_____

_____

What conditions do we impose on ourselves in regard to forgiveness of sin?

_____

_____

9. Do you believe this prayer was intended to be repeated, or is it a model on which to fashion our own prayer life?

_____

_____

10. Are we dependent on times, places and forms for our prayer life?

_____

_____

11. What are some of the times and places for prayer?

_____

_____

15
Giving

1. Under the Jewish Dispensation, how was religious work supported? (Leviticus 27:30-33)

_____

_____

_____

_____

_____

2. What has God done to place us under obligation to give to His work? (James 1:17; Romans 5:16-18; 6:23)

_____

_____

_____

_____

_____

3. What is the first gift required of the Christian? (2 Corinthians 8:5)

_____

_____

_____

_____

4. Which is more important—the amount we give or the proportion that we give? (Mark 12:41-44)

_____

_____

5. Check as true or false the following statements against 1 Corinthians 16:2.

_____ We should give only when the cause appeals to us.

_____ We should have a regular system of giving.

_____ We should depend on bake sales, suppers, etc., to support the church.

_____ Everyone should give the same amount.

_____ The amount we give should depend on our prosperity.

_____ Every one should pay dues to the church like those paid to clubs or lodges.

6. What should be the spirit of giving? (Matthew 10:8; 2 Corinthians 9:6)

_____

_____

_____

7. What is a steward? _____

_____

_____

_____

8. What does the parable of Jesus, in Matthew 25:14-30, teach about our possessions?

_____

_____

_____

_____

9. Does the church have an obligation to the poor? (Acts 6:1-4; Galatians 2:10; 1 John 3:17; James 1:27)

_____

_____

10. How are gifts for the poor to be given? (Matthew 6:1-4)

_____

_____

_____

11. What is the sin we commit when we withhold offerings from God? (Malachi 3:8-10)

_____

_____

_____

Key Words

Using your dictionary, give a definition of the following:

Tithe _____

_____

_____

Stewardship _____

_____

_____

Parable _____

_____

_____

Devil _____

_____

16

The Growth of Christian Character

1. When we become Christians what is our position in the family of God? (1 Peter 2:2, 3)

_____

_____

_____

2. What should be our aim in the Christian life? (1 John 2:6; 1 Peter 2:21)

_____

_____

_____

_____

_____

_____

3. We are justified by faith. What are the steps of development after faith? (2 Peter 1:5-7)

_____

_____

_____

_____

4. What is to be our aim after we have mastered the first principles of doctrine? (Hebrews 6:1)

_____

_____

_____

_____

_____

5. While striving for perfection, is it necessary for us to reach it in order to be Christians? (Philippians 3:12-15)

_____

_____

_____

_____

6. What help toward growth in grace have you found in your Bible reading during this course?

_____

_____

_____

_____

_____

7. Do you believe you can grow in Christian character without prayer, worship, the Holy Spirit and regular Bible reading? Discuss briefly from your former lessons.

_____

_____

_____

_____

_____

8. What is the highest motive that we can have in dealing with our fellow men? (John 15:12; 13:34, 35; Matthew 19:19; Luke 6:35)

_____

_____

9. Why is the motive of love so essential for the Christian? (Ephesians 5:2; 1 John 4:19)

_____

_____

_____

_____

10. What kind of action is prompted by love? (Matthew 25:31-46; John 13:2-17; Luke 6:31)

_____

_____

_____

Key Words

Using your dictionary, find meanings for the following:

Covet _____

_____

_____

Worldly _____

_____

_____

Temptation _____

_____

_____

Abomination _____

_____

17
Worship

1. What is worship? _____
_____

2. On a separate sheet of paper outline the order of worship used in your local church. If your church has a bulletin, you will find it there.

3. After each of the parts of the service in the following, (a) tell why you think it is a suitable part of worship; and (b) what *you should do* or *what your attitude should be* in order that you may worship.

(1) The Invocation.

(a) _____
_____

(b) _____
_____

(2) Singing of Hymns.

(a) _____
_____

(b) _____
_____

(3) The Minister's Prayer.

(a) _____
_____

(b) _____

_____

(4) The Reading of the Scriptures.

(a) _____

_____

(b) _____

_____

(5) The Offering.

(a) _____

_____

(b) _____

_____

(6) The Sermon.

(a) _____

_____

(b) _____

_____

(7) The Communion Service.

(a) _____

_____

(b) _____

_____

4. Which of these things do you consider the most important?

_____

Why? _____

_____

_____

5. What did Jesus say was essential to true worship? (John 4:23.)

_____

_____

6. Are the forms of worship acceptable to God without a proper spirit? (Amos 5:21-24; Luke 18:9-14)

_____

_____

7. How should you prepare yourself for the worship service? Are visiting and talking before the service a detriment?

_____

_____

8. Can one worship God in places other than the church?

_____

_____

9. Do people who stay away from church and claim to worship on the golf course, on the lake, etc., usually worship, or do they play golf, fish, etc.?

_____

_____

10. Are we commanded to assemble, or may worship always be private? (Hebrews 10:24, 25)

_____

_____

_____

11. What provision have you made for private worship?

_____

_____

18

Your Local Church

[To obtain the answers to these questions you should interview the treasurer, clerk, chairman of the board, sunday school superintendent, pastor, etc.]

1. What is the name of your local church?

_____

2. When was it organized?

_____

3. How many members does it have?

_____

4. How many elders does it have? _____

How many deacons? _____

5. How are these elected? _____

_____

_____

6. When is the annual congregational meeting held?

7. How much of the annual budget is for current expenses?

_____

8. How is this money raised?

_____

_____

_____

_____

9. Give some reasons why you should attend the congregational meetings.

_____

_____

10. How much money does your church give to missions? _____

11. Where does this money go?

_____

_____

_____

_____

12. How many are enrolled in your sunday school?

_____

13. How many teachers are there in your sunday school?

_____

_____

14. How does one qualify to be a teacher?

_____

_____

_____

15. What Christian journals or magazines does your minister recommend that you read?

_____

_____

16. Does your church have various organized groups to do special kinds of work? (Missionary Society, Boy Scouts, Men's Fellowship, Women's Fellowship, etc.) If it does, name the ones you would be eligible to participate in.

_____

_____

17. When you move to a new community, what should you do about your church membership?

_____

_____

18. How do you proceed to move your membership?

_____

_____

_____

Key Words

Use your dictionary to find the meaning of these words:

Advocate _____

_____

_____

Atonement _____

_____

_____

Sacrifice _____

_____

19
My Part in the Local Church

1. Prepare a list of the meetings held by your church. In one word or phrase, such as "Worship," "Bible Study," "Prayer," etc., describe each meeting. If this meeting serves some need of yours, mark what that need is.

Name and Time of Meeting	Purpose of Meeting	Personal Need Met

2. List hobbies, special interests and abilities which you believe you possess.

3. How can you use these talents in the work of your church?

_____

_____

_____

4. What work in the church would you like to undertake without any further training?

_____

_____

_____

_____

_____

5. For what work in the church would you like to begin training yourself?

_____

_____

_____

_____

_____

6. How will you go about training yourself for this work?

_____

_____

_____

_____

_____

7. Should every Christian be a contributor to the work of the church? (1 Corinthians 16:2)

_____

_____

_____

8. Should every Christian be an evangelist? (2 Corinthians 4:13; 1 Peter 3:15; Luke 8:39; 2 Timothy 1:8)

_____

_____

_____

_____

_____

9. What work do you see that you can do as a personal evangelist?

_____

_____

_____

_____

10. What kind of projects (ministries) does your church need that it does not now have?

_____

_____

_____

_____

_____

20
Life and Teaching of Christ

[During your course you should read the Gospel of Mark and fill out the incomplete statements that follow. Mark's Gospel is the shortest of the four Gospels, but will give you valuable insight into the life and teaching of Jesus the Christ. Begin at the beginning and read until you find the answer to the first question. Then read until you find the answer to the second question, and continue this way until you have completed the book. Be careful to answer all questions. The answers should be found in the same order in the book as the questions appear in your lessons. Please notice that you are here introduced to many questions that are not covered by our study, such as marriage and divorce, the second coming of Christ, etc. You might make a note of such topics for future study.]

Chapter 1

1. John the Baptist preached the baptism of _____

_____

2. When Jesus was baptized the Voice from heaven said, "_____

_____"

3. Jesus was tempted for _____ days by _____ .

4. Jesus preached, "The time has come, the _____ of God is near, _____ and believe

the _____ _____"

5. Jesus called four men. Their names were _____ , _____ ,

_____ and _____

6. Jesus taught them as one who had _____ , not as the _____

7. Jesus performed a miracle on Simon's _____

8. In Capernaum, Jesus healed those sick of _____ and

those possessed of _____

9. Jesus arose before it was day and departed into a solitary place to _____

10. Jesus could not enter a town at this time because _____

_____

Chapter 2

11. The reason given by Jesus for curing the paralytic man was "that you may know _____"

12. Jesus said to Levi, "_____"

13. Jesus came not to call the _____ but _____

14. Jesus taught that the time was coming when the bridegroom would be _____ ,

and on that day the disciples would _____

15. Jesus taught that the Son of man was Lord of _____

_____

Chapter 3

16. Jesus was deeply distressed at the people's stubborn _____

17. Those with evil spirits cried, saying "_____

_____"

18. Jesus chose twelve disciples, named:

_____   _____   _____   _____

_____   _____   _____   _____

_____   _____   _____   _____

19. Jesus taught there was an eternal sin because the teachers of the law said, "He has _____"

20. Jesus said, "Whoever does _____ is

my brother and sister and mother."

Chapter 4

21. In this parable there are four kinds of soil; they are

(1) _____ (2) _____ (3) _____

(4) _____

22. In the parable of the sower, the seed is the _____

and the soils represent _____

23. The kingdom is like growing grain. It has first _____ ,

then _____ , and finally the _____

24. The kingdom is like a grain of mustard seed; it begins as the smallest of all _____ and grows to be

the greatest of all _____. _____

25. When Jesus stilled the storm the disciples said, "_____

_____"

Chapter 5

26. The man with an evil spirit called Jesus, "_____

_____"

27. Jesus sent the man who had been possessed of demons to preach to _____

and to tell them _____

28. Jairus desired that Jesus should put His hands on his daughter that she might _____

29. When the woman who was subject to bleeding touched His garment, Jesus realized that _____

30. When the daughter of the ruler of the synagogue died, Jesus said to the father, "_____ ;

just _____"

Chapter 6

31. Jesus' brothers were named _____ , _____ ,

_____ and _____

32. When the Twelve were sent forth they preached that "people _____

_____"

33. Herod beheaded John the Baptist because "_____

_____"

34. Jesus divided _____ loaves and _____ fishes

among _____ men and there were _____ basketfuls left.

35. Jesus walked on the lake to His disciples and said, "_____

_____"

36. In Gennesaret as many as touched the _____

were _____

Chapter 7

37. Jesus taught that nothing outside _____ of a man can _____ but the

things that came out of a man, those things can _____

38. Because of the faith of a Syrophoenician woman her _____

had a _____ cast out of her by Jesus.

39. After the healing of the deaf mute the crowd was astonished, saying, "_____"

Chapter 8

40. Jesus fed _____ people with seven _____ and a few _____ and

_____ basketfuls were left.

41. The Pharisees were seeking a _____ from heaven.

42. Jesus said, "Be careful, watch out for _____ and that of Herod."

43. The blind man first saw people as _____ .

44. When Jesus asked who He was, Peter answered, "_____

_____

45. "If anyone is _____ of _____ and my _____

in this adulterous and sinful generation, the Son of man will be ashamed of him, _____

in his Father's glory with the holy angels."

Chapter 9

46. There came a voice from the cloud, saying, "_____

_____ "

47. Jesus instructed the disciples they were to tell no one of His transfiguration until _____

48. The father of the boy said, "I _____ ; help me _____ "

49. Jesus prophesied that sinful men would _____ Him

and after _____ He would _____

50. "Whoever welcomes one of these little children _____ welcomes

me: whoever welcomes me, does not welcome _____ but

the one _____ "

51. "Anyone who gives you a cup of water in my name because _____

_____ will certainly not _____ "

Chapter 10

52. "Anyone who divorces his wife and marries another woman _____

_____ and if she divorces her husband and marries another man, she _____ "

53. Anyone who will not receive the _____ like a little child will never _____ "

54. The young man was sad because _____

_____

55. How hard is it for _____ to

enter the _____

56. The Son of man will be betrayed to _____

they will _____ and will hand Him over to _____

who will _____

three days later He will _____

57. Whoever wants to become great among the disciples must be _____

_____ , and whoever wants to be first must be _____

58. Jesus said of Bartimaeus, "Your _____ has _____"

Chapter 11

59. The multitude, at the time of the triumphal entry, hailed Jesus as _____

60. When the priests and the teachers of the law hear that _____

_____ they began looking for a way to kill Him.

61. When we pray we should _____ so that our Father

in Heaven may _____

62. The chief priests, teachers of the law and elders wanted to know by _____

_____

Chapter 12

63. In illustrating the way men have treated God's messengers, Jesus said that they _____ the servants

and _____ the Son.

64. We are to give to Caesar _____ ,

and to God _____

65. They that rise from the dead do not _____ nor

are they _____

66. The greatest commandment is _____

_____

and the second is this: _____

67. The _____ listened to Him _____

68. The poor widow's gift was most acceptable because she gave _____

Chapter 13

69. Jesus foretold that there would be _____
_____ , but that these things
were not the end, but the beginning of birth pains.

70. The followers of Jesus can expect _____
_____ in this world.

71. We are to be on guard that we are not led astray by _____
_____

72. Jesus will come to earth again to _____
_____

73. The time of His coming is not known by _____ , but is known by _____

74. Since we do not know the time of Christ's coming we are to _____ lest we be found _____

Chapter 14

75. The purpose of the anointing at Bethany was that Jesus might be anointed _____
for His _____

76. While Judas made ready to _____ Jesus made ready to eat _____

77. Jesus knew that one of the _____ who _____ would betray Him.

78. In instituting the Lord's Supper, Jesus gave His disciples _____ to represent His _____
and a cup to represent His _____

79. Peter was very sure that he would not _____ ,
but Jesus said, "Before the rooster crows twice, you yourself will _____ "

80. Jesus prayed _____ times that He would not have to drink the cup of sorrow, but He also prayed,

"Yet not what I _____ but _____"

81. Judas pointed Jesus out to the soldiers by _____

82. The disciples and those that followed all _____

83. At the trial the high priest asked, "Are you the _____

_____ ," and Jesus answered, "_____"

84. Peter denied that _____ and to enforce this denial he began to _____ and he _____

Chapter 15

85. Pilate asked, "Are you the _____ ," and Jesus answered, "_____"

86. Pilate gave the people a choice between _____ and _____ , and the people asked to

have _____

released and Jesus _____

87. Before the soldiers crucified Jesus they _____

_____

88. The cross of Jesus was carried by _____

89. When Jesus was on the cross the chief priest said, "He _____

_____ , but he can't _____"

90. The centurion who had charge of the crucifixion said of Jesus, "_____"

91. Jesus was buried by _____ in a _____

and a _____ was rolled against the door.

Chapter 16

92. On the _____ of the week the women came to anoint the body.

93. The women saw an angel in the empty tomb who told them _____

_____

94. Jesus appeared first to _____

95. Jesus appeared to two disciples, who told the rest, but they did not _____

96. Jesus commissioned His followers to preach in _____

97. After the resurrection Jesus was taken _____

and sat at the _____

_____

Notes

Notes

Notes

Notes

Notes

Notes

Notes

Notes

Notes